PPING POODLE STANDING BIRTHDAYS BAGPIPES QE2 SUMO
LERBLADING LOVERS WEDDINGS FOG LAMPOSTS VERTIGO
OLIS SHADOW BLIMPS ALPACAS EXHA W9-CTQ-355 LDREN
GPIPES QE2 SUMO KANGAROO IBIS C SURFER
MPOSTS VERTIGO TRAINS TRIATHLON SALAD DAYS GRAFFITI
VE CHILDREN DANCING CAT NAPPING POODLE STANDING
WINDSURFER CYCLISTS NUDE ROLLERBLADING LOVERS
AD DAYS GRAFFITI BAOBAB METROPOLIS SHADOW BLIMPS
NG POODLE STANDING BIRTHDAYS BAGPIPES QE2 SUMO
LERBLADING LOVERS WEDDINGS FOG LAMPOSTS VERTIGO
OLIS SHADOW BLIMPS ALPACAS EXHAUSTS FIVE CHILDREN
GPIPES QE2 SUMO KANGAROO IBIS CANON WINDSURFER
MPOSTS VERTIGO TRAINS TRIATHLON SALAD DAYS GRAFFITI
VE CHILDREN DANCING CAT NAPPING POODLE STANDING
WINDSURFER CYCLISTS NUDE ROLLERBLADING LOVERS
AD DAYS GRAFFITI BAOBAB METROPOLIS SHADOW BLIMPS
NG POODLE STANDING BIRTHDAYS BAGPIPES QE2 SUMO
LERBLADING LOVERS WEDDINGS FOG LAMPOSTS VERTIGO
OLIS SHADOW BLIMPS ALPACAS EXHAUSTS FIVE CHILDREN
GPIPES QE2 SUMO KANGAROO IBIS CANON WINDSURFER
MPOSTS VERTIGO TRAINS TRIATHLON SALAD DAYS GRAFFITI
VE CHILDREN DANCING CAT NAPPING POODLE STANDING
WINDSURFER CYCLISTS NUDE ROLLERBLADING LOVERS
AD DAYS GRAFFITI BAOBAB METROPOLIS SHADOW BLIMPS

THE
BRIDGE

Twilight deepens. The North Shore heights are a silhouette of purple, and headland, beach and bay merge into a vague background of shadows and uncertain darkness. The great arch of the Bridge is limned against the clouds like the skeleton of some prehistoric giant, a million bleached bones reflecting the light of a darkening sky.

Extract from "Cameos of Sydney: The Harbour"
by Georgina Little
Sydney Mail, Wednesday January 3, 1934, page 46

THE
BRIDGE

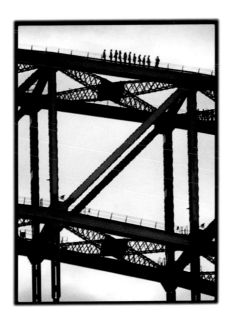

Photographs by Robert Billington • Text by Sarah Billington

Foreword by Giles Auty

PERIBO
PUBLISHERS OF FINE BOOKS

Cycle Way – No Pedestrians

FOREWORD

Sydney Harbour Bridge is rare among public monuments in Australia in being referred to only occasionally by its nickname – the coathanger – and never being shrunk verbally, unlike the mighty Melbourne Cricket Ground, merely to the sum of its initials.

I like to believe Sydney Harbour Bridge is too magnificent and awe-inspiring for such treatment. Whatever else gets built in Sydney, the Harbour Bridge will remain my favourite landmark, whether looming unexpectedly through a gap between buildings or glimpsed distantly from a boat or jetty. Have you seen the bridge silhouetted by a summer sunset yet from Watson's Bay ?

For residents who have been away from Sydney for any length of time, a first sighting of the Harbour Bridge provides reassurance that they are really home at last. The Harbour Bridge has been a silent witness to the events of over two-thirds of our century, a time of phenomenal and accelerated change.

By now we have attained an extraordinary self-confidence in our technical abilities, yet doubts remain whether we could – or would – ever build a bridge again in quite such a massive and enduring-looking manner. To be frank, I admire the bridge for its unashamed look of purpose and ruggedness. More beautiful edifices exist but the bridge somehow encapsulates a lot of the best, old-fashioned Australian virtues. Although expertise from overseas paved its path, many of its huge components were built or assembled on home soil. Among the overlooked virtues of the bridge is the amount of work its building generated locally at a time of desperate unemployment and painful recession. An average of 1,400 people were employed continuously during the 8 years the Harbour Bridge took to construct between 1924 and 1932. Their wages also helped to keep a much wider community going in a time of want.

Because of my great affection for the bridge, I was pleased especially to be asked to write words of introduction to this book of Robert Billington's photographs of the subject. If I were more skilful or industrious these are just the kind of photographs I would like to have taken myself.

I, too, have always wielded a camera, although my own first professional career was that of painter – long before I entertained any thought of becoming an art critic or coming to work in Australia. Composition is probably the element that binds painting and photography together most closely. Good painters make composition a major priority, and fine photographers such as Robert Billington clearly do the same. Composition gives balance and excitement to black and white photographs especially and creates what is best described as 'pictorial tension' – the sense that not a single pictorial element can be moved or changed without a major loss to the whole. However, this is not an appropriate place to go into the technical intricacies of photography.

Here is a book to be enjoyed, among other things, for the simple memories it conjures up of the most dominant feature of Australia's largest city. I doubt whether any more complete memento or keepsake than this book exists for true enthusiasts of one of the great relics of 1920s engineering.

Robert Billington explores the object of a long-term personal passion in all its moods, and does so through the eyes of a poet in his medium. He senses poetic potential where others might see only the prosaic. The poetry of the subject steals in on days of fog and rain no less than on those of high, bright clouds, sunshine and dense shadows.

Unlike the case with much of Australia, there is a winter in Sydney, days on which bare trees in Lower Fort Street – one prominent approach to the bridge – might well have reminded certain pre-war immigrants a little of their birthplaces in Glasgow, Birmingham or London. Then a parakeet, ibis or pelican would fly overhead and the illusion would vanish.

Today, it is easy to forget how much scale has changed since the earlier epochs of the Harbour Bridge. Once it was surrounded at its southern end only by prim Victorian or Edwardian housing, with little above three storeys even in the way of light industrial buildings or hotels.

While first thinking about writing this essay, I wandered by chance past the Harbour View Hotel, completed in 1922, whose claims to any panorama were soon to be dashed by the building of the southern approaches to the bridge. At the time of my wandering, the hotel was being renovated with its stucco front repainted bravely in cream and turquoise. It was as though time had stood still and we remained in the days following the First World War when many a seaside hotel was painted in these precise, cheery colours.

The Harbour Bridge and its surrounds are replete with the ghosts of Australian history. In 1900 an unfortunate wharfie contracted the plague and a whole area of cramped and possibly insanitary housing was peremptorily swept away. Subsequent demolitions in Sydney have not always happened for so compelling a reason.

Yet, the Harbour Bridge has also involved vital demolitions of its own. In order to be able to fabricate necessary steelwork on site, the original Milsons Point railway station had to be pulled down. But when the Harbour Bridge was completed its onsite steelworks gave way, in turn, to the Luna Park funfair complex – a place of often unsuspected significance in the courtships of many Sydneysiders. Yet today even Luna Park's Big Wheel – always an excellent excuse for closer clingings as its seats neared their zenith – is dwarfed by the massive but workaday high-rise office blocks of North Sydney.

From sites below the approaches to the bridge, trains clatter overhead, leading the eye up to a jumbo jet sometimes, straining skywards while carrying enough passengers to populate a village. How technology and foreign travel have changed since the early years of the Harbour Bridge and the heyday of the great ocean liners which once docked in its shadow. But the romance of the glory days still lingers somehow. By being close to the Harbour Bridge, visitors may hope legitimately that some of the historic glamour might rub off. The surrounds are as good a place as any for lovers who seek to create indelible memories… remember that day when we strolled by the Sydney Harbour Bridge ?

For the moment, at least, their lives took place on a natural film set.

.   .   .

In spite of my resolution not to write about photographic techniques, what could make a more appropriate front cover for this book than a view which relies for its impact on a telephoto lens ? The shot itself looks rather like a still from a film and emphasises the non-stop bustle of the bridge. It is easy to forget sometimes that the Harbour Bridge was built to be used rather than merely looked at.

When Sydney Harbour Bridge opened in March 1932 it carried an average of only 11,000 vehicles a day. There was probably not even a noise enough from these to drown the roars of disapproval from 'the Hill' at Sydney Cricket Ground when the infamous Bodyline series opened there in December of that year – if the wind were blowing from the right direction, that is.

Today the Sydney Harbour Bridge carries 20 times that amount of traffic. Did its builders foresee this or imagine what life – or people – would really be like at the turn of the century ? Who could ever have imagined that a building so outwardly eccentric as the Sydney Opera House might one day sit alongside the Harbour Bridge and rival its attraction ?

Will the complex new stadium built for the Olympics at Homebush ever achieve the iconic status of the pair of structures which represented the resurgent optimism of the aftermaths of two world wars ? Will the stadium ever inspire paintings as full of futuristic hope as those Grace Cossington-Smith once made of the then incomplete Sydney Harbour Bridge ?

In its day the Sydney Harbour Bridge represented a rebirth of confidence of considerable proportions. If some of the hopes – such as that for prolonged worldwide peace – proved destined for disappointment, at least Australian hearts still seemed in the right place. Building the Harbour Bridge, in the economic climate of the time, demanded – in the local vernacular – a good deal of 'ticker'.

Perhaps what I like most about the Harbour Bridge is the reminder it provides of an age of lost innocence when our century still seemed a time of unlimited human as well as technical potential. When my late father was a boy he did not watch television or play video games – neither yet existed – but swam and studied hard and practised like mad at his local cricket nets. The world of the Harbour Bridge's own infancy was harsh and tough for many yet also simple and less confusing in its aims than our current climate.

The world in which the Harbour Bridge grew to its own adulthood was one of frequent want and workaday toughness, spiced with fellowship and much good humour. For some people – of whom I hope you may be one – Sydney Harbour Bridge provides a touchstone to an almost forgotten world.

•   •   •

Like me, Robert Billington was born in England but unlike me has spent most of his working life in Australia. One effect of a transition from a very different continent is that the new one retains its aura of mystery and excitement with particular potency. Australia, as a whole, is a visual banquet but this fact can be forgotten sometimes by those who were born sitting at the table.

A major part of the enchantment of this book of photographs lies in the endless freshness of its maker's approach. Too much 'artistic' photography deals in artistic cliché. By contrast, this book provided me with endless fun as I leafed through image after image, many of which caused me to smile inwardly – or even to laugh out loud.

Two cats sit on a table awkwardly, uncertain of whether they should really be there or not. At the precise moment the photographer prepares to shoot, one cat decides to remove itself altogether. But that is cats for you – they are constitutionally unwilling to let themselves be arranged. In the far distance lies the Harbour Bridge and one is persuaded that this is an entirely natural moment in the life of Australia's Harbour City. What we are seeing is not artifice but artistry.

Although reflections are a photographer's standby, some of those in this book have the bizarre appearance of happening simply by chance. The photographer also looks to have been tremendously lucky with animals – a tied up dog turns to look at him in one shot while, in others, dogs seemingly disregard him completely, having their own personal business to fulfil.

Not absolutely every image features the Harbour Bridge. Sometimes we look out from its unique standpoint, so that the bridge forms only an unseen presence – as when half a dozen ibises fly by. At other times we deal, unsurprisingly, with the iron guts of the bridge and with those vertigo-free pedestrians who traverse its upper walkways – with official permission, of course.

In my first career, I was largely a painter of landscapes. Artists who have long experience of this genre of painting may tell you that after many hours staring at a particular piece of landscape, they experience the uncanny sensation that the landscape is staring back at them – perhaps to weigh up their fitness for the particular task they have set themselves.

If this odd illusion happens also to photographers, I like to think that when Robert Billington stares next at the Sydney Harbour Bridge, he will sense some secret sign of its approval.

Giles Auty

Stairs from Cumberland Street, The Rocks

Maintenance workers' picnic table

'Bob Menzies' graffiti

Bridge Stairs, Kirribilli

Bridge Stairs, The Rocks

11

Here we may stand, and see the blue waves dance,
Where Arthur Phillip watched with eyes of dreams,
The wooded shore and desolate expanse,
Of sea that bore no life, and then, perchance,
Looked down the years and saw, as daybreak gleams,
After the sombre night, this loveliness –
Meet recompense for all the long duress.

And those may see, who keep God's Vision yet,
The gallant ones who fought for this great day,
Whose feet of old in barren ways were set,
Who saw the gold where dark clouds formed and met,
Where lesser souls had only seen the grey,
All praise to them who toiled the long years through,
That we might see their splendid dream come true !

The Bridge Opening

by Nellie A. Evans

The Sydney Morning Herald, Saturday March 19, 1932, page 9

13

9 a.m. Sunday

Cumberland Street, The Rocks

The Great Day is close upon us. The day when North Sydney and the City of Sydney will be officially linked. They are already materially and physically linked, but officially they are asunder. It only requires a little ceremony, and the two great centres of population will be indissolubly joined.

The Premier of the State is to do the joining. Mr Lang will make a snick with a pair of scissors, and the great work of Dorman, Long, and Co. will be officially consummated. This Bridge of Bridges will then be at the will of the public. They may walk over it, they may drive over it (provided they pay the poll tax), or they may run over it. However they may choose to cross it need not concern anyone. The people on the North side have been paying for it, are paying for it, and will be paying for it till 1939. Who in the Northern Suburbs doesn't wish for the advent of 1939?

This does not seem to be a political question, nor has anyone sought to make it a political question. Neither is it a City question, nor a suburban question. The bridge belongs to the State. But in its incidence it affects the people on the Northern side of the Harbour more, perhaps, than any other section of the community. They have a more immediate interest in the bridge than the boundary rider out Tibooboora way or the dam sinker on the plains of Mamre.

And why shouldn't these people of the Northern Suburbs jubilate over the opening of a World's Greatest Bridge in which they have so vital an interest ? They are ready for the great opening ceremony. Unlike the five foolish virgins, they have not been slumbering and sleeping while the bridegroom tarried. They are wide-awake for the bridal morn. The oil in their lamps is burning. They are ready to go out to meet the bridegroom. They have been preparing for his coming for months past. Their programme for Bridge Week is a stupendous affair.

Extract from "North Sydney Bridge Week"
The Great Northern Bridge Opening Souvenir, Friday March 18, 1932, page 10

17

Rollerblader on Cycle Way, looking to the north

18

"The Arcadia", Millers Point

7 a.m. Sunday

Bob Young of Manly was paying his toll at the Harbour Bridge on Monday night when the toll collector surprised him by reaching through the open window and lighting the cigarette he had in his mouth. Mr Young wonders whether this was simply the toll collector's way of paying tribute to his 1949 Bentley.

From The Sydney Morning Herald, May 13, 1981, page 1

Wedding car viewed from The Palisade, Millers Point

If you come often to Sydney via the Bridge
And have studied the racing notes
And scanned the headlines,
You may glance at the Cables
Or the crimson painted nails
of the woman opposite.
But, if you have not passed that way before,
You will look at the Pylons
And you will say to yourself:
'How regular these pinnacles are,
And
How alien!'
And, when they are behind,
'I am treading upon the smoke
Of a ship that perhaps
Sailed out from Brazil;'
Or you will whisper to yourself:
'This is the way the winds walk
Above the sea.
Where the gulls flicker like silver moths.'

Then you will want to put your hands
Out of the window
And let them flutter
With all the things
That move above the waters.
And, when you are in the centre –
That enormous centre
Moulded of concrete and steel,
And the sweat of hands
And the labour of minds –
And there is nothing beneath
But the wind and the smoke and the gulls –
Nothing to the East and nothing to the West
But the miraculous web of the skies
Spun from the four horizons,
'This is a great wonder,'
Your spirit will sing:
'I shall not pass
This way again, too soon,
That I may keep
This vast astonishment'.

Via the Bridge

by Ricketty Kate (Minnie Agnes Filson)

Back of Holden ute

Bridge by night

Cycle Way north and south

Though the Bridge toll system worked splendidly yesterday, scores of people caused delay by presenting £10, £5, and £1 notes. One woman in a new Buick car presented a £50 note. The collector refused it, and there was a hold-up while she fumbled in her bag for the correct fare.

Tollmen Faced a £50 Note

The Daily Telegraph, Monday March 21, 1932, page 3

Mid summer – out of the car window

9.30 a.m. Tuesday, looking north

That sombre day when somebody actually starves to death in a traffic jam may have edged a trifle closer during Sydney's mammoth kilometres-long North Shore snarl on Monday. But, happily, catastrophe was averted for two computer engineers stuck on the Bridge. Almost overcome with hunger, the City-bound technicians spotted a motionless delivery truck sharing their lane. It was the work of an instant to get the truck open for business. And soon chocolate biscuits were sustaining the trapped and starving motorists.

From The Sydney Morning Herald, September 2, 1981, page 1

View to Kent Street carpark

One superstitious motorist we know of has been concerned about the danger of driving through the number 13 tollgate on the Harbour Bridge. The 19 toll booths on the Bridge do, indeed, have numbers, although except for those on the northern side of the Bridge, they cannot easily be seen. We discovered yesterday, however, that there is no number 13 booth. The booths are numbered one to 12 and 14 to 20. According to the Department of Main Roads spokesman, this is not to please the superstitious. "It just happened that the number 13 booth was removed some years ago and the others have not been renumbered," he said.

View of Pier One, Dawes Point

Argyle Street steps, Observatory Park

Cycle Way and windsurfer, looking north

The Government is to take steps immediately to make the pedestrian pathways on the Harbour Bridge proof against persons desirous of committing suicide. Ministers take a serious view of the increasing number of suicides from the bridge, which now total 38.

The Cabinet decided yesterday to instruct the Main Roads Board to have an effective barrier erected on the pedestrian pathways. It is proposed to erect a small mesh wire along the railings, and a wire frame on the top, projecting over the footway. More than four miles of wire will be used in the work. The Premier (Mr Stevens) said it was felt that something must be done urgently, if lives were to be saved.

Harbour Bridge to Be Made Suicide Proof – Barriers to Be Built

From The Sydney Morning Herald, November 22, 1933

Premier Bob Carr yesterday presided over a shameful episode in the State's history as he allowed a gloating Queensland Premier Peter Beattie to hoist his State's flag above our bridge. The end point of a silly bet between the two men, Queensland's gloating ensign will hang on the hanger for 48 hours to remind future state leaders not to agree to rash bets on the State of Origin outcome. Not even a 200-step climb or the winds and rain at the summit of the south pylon could dampen Beattie's glee as he watched his "great icon" being hoisted above the harbour. 'At last Sydney has a landmark it can be proud of,' he quipped (rather poorly). 'I would like to point out that whenever there is a Labor government in Queensland and New South Wales, Queensland always wins the Origin.'

Meanwhile, riggers who'd threatened to disrupt the flag raising in protest at threatened public sector job cuts were bribed into submission by the gift of a NSW Origin jersey autographed by the team.

Ultimate Shame

From The Sydney Morning Herald's 'Stay in Touch' column,
Tuesday 29 June, 1999

Queensland State Flag viewed from South East Pylon

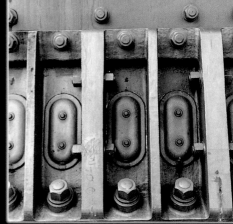

Bridge details – Dawes Point and Milsons Point

The Sydney Harbour Bridge is held together by rivets only. There are no welded or bolted joints essential to the main structure.

There are approximately 6 million rivets in the Bridge, adding a total of approximately 3,200 tonnes to the weight. The largest rivet is 371 mm long by 36 mm in diameter and it was at the time the largest rivet ever used in a steel structure. The smallest rivet is 32 mm long and 17 mm in diameter.

McPhersons Pty Ltd supplied all the rivets for the Bridge under contract to Dorman, Long and Co. Ltd. To ensure the rivets would withstand heavy loads, a system of quality control was established. Two or three rivets were chosen at random from each batch and tested to the recommended levels. All of the rivets were manufactured in Australia.

McPhersons Pty.Ltd. of Melbourne

From "The Story of the Sydney Harbour Bridge", page 21

Mr Lawrence Ennis, 'a big man who did a big job,' has confessed to stress of emotion at the critical stage when the half-arches were about to meet. It was night-time. He was unable to speak as the parts joined and settled into place. Then, after some little time, he said: "Well, boys, that's that, and thank God she is home." Those present shook hands. They had achieved something that many engineers in various parts of the world had said was impossible.

Extract from "Mr Lawrence Ennis: The Builder of the Bridge"

Sydney Mail: Special Bridge Number, Wednesday March 16, 1932, page 16

OPPOSITE: Milsons Point

Bridge climb

Inclusive of the approaches the total length of the bridge is 2³/₄ miles.

To make provision for the effect of heat and cold, allowance has been made for a deck expansion of 16¹/₂ inches.

The height of the pylons is 285 ft above mean sea-level.

There are 300 lamp and lantern fittings on the bridge and approaches, and over 100,000 lineal feet of conduit has been used in the electric wiring to supply them with current.

Twenty thousand cubic yards of granite – all obtained from Moruya – were required for the facing of the piers and pylons.

As an instance of the expense incurred in 'incidentals' in the construction of the bridge, it may be mentioned that the cost of erecting the two 'creeper' cranes in position was upwards of £30,000, exclusive of the cost of the cranes themselves.

If the Sydney GPO were placed on the centre of the bridge decking, the top of its tower (which is 252 ft from the ground level) would rise only 2 ft above the top chord of the arch.

The top of the tower of the Post Office, the top of the flagstaff on the Sydney Church of England Grammar School at North Sydney ('Shore'), and the tops of the pylons of the bridge are all at approximately the same height above sea-level.

Some Salient Points

Sydney Mail: Special Bridge Number, Wednesday March 16, 1932, page 4

Maintenance workers

Vertigo

Australia's first Luna Park was opened at St.Kilda, Melbourne, in 1912, by the American showmen, the Phillips brothers and J.J. Williams. Another entrepreneurial showman of the time, David Atkins, saw how the park grew in popularity during the Depression and convinced the Phillips brothers to open another at the seaside town of Glenelg, in South Australia, in 1930.

Initially it was a success but, five years later, when the developers wanted to expand the fun fair and make the joy rides bigger, they ran up against opposition from nearby residents and the local council, which refused to give permission for any further development.

If you can't beat 'em, leave 'em, was Atkins' attitude, so he proceeded to have the whole show dismantled, carefully numbered and packed on to a large barge, which then began its long, slow, careful journey around and up the coast to Sydney and a 2.6 ha vacant lot at Milson's Point.

There, on the edge of the harbor, underneath the just opened and already world famous Sydney Harbour Bridge, it was all unloaded onto the wharf on which the Dodgem Building would soon stand.

In 1935, the Depression was biting hard into the spirit of Sydneysiders. The completion of the bridge had been cause to celebrate but July's winter chill, long dole queues and packed soup kitchens had taken away much of the joy.

No sooner had the barge entered the harbor than many of the men who had built the bridge were at the jetty, ready to unpack and reassemble the bits and pieces of another of Sydney's landmarks – a place on the water that was to be Just For Fun.

He was a 'nice chap,' the man who put the smile on Luna Park – Lovable Arthur Barton

From Sunday Telegraph, Sunday, January 19,1992, page 129

Luna Park reflection

OPPOSITE: North Sydney Pool

View from McMahons Point

There is no possibility of the Harbor Bridge collapsing when the big weight test is made on February 7, said Dr Bradfield yesterday.

The heavy load of railway engines will be placed on the Bridge, he said, merely to ascertain the stresses and strains of the sections.

Weight Test, Will Not Crash Bridge

The Daily Telegraph, Saturday, January 9, 1932, page 1

53

View from McMahons Point

To-day two points of Port Jackson, which are known to us as Dawes Point and Milson's Point, are united by a web of steel, and one may, if one has the inclination, walk from one point to the other. The names of these two places come from two men, each, in his way, a remarkable man, and the union of the two points provides a fitting opportunity to bring these men again onto the scene.

Dawes was an, explorer, mapmaker, student of language, of anthropology, of astronomy, of botany, of surveying and of engineering, teacher and philanthropist. There is little doubt that it was scientific curiosity and philanthropy which prompted Dawes to seek a place in the First Fleet to set out for these shores, and when an opportunity arose in July, 1788, to transfer from the ship's books to the marines, he eagerly accepted it so that he could remain in a country which gave him a virgin field for his scientific labours.

At the suggestion of the Astronomer Royal of England, the Rev. Dr. Maskelyne, Lieutenant Dawes had been furnished with the necessary astronomical instruments, and his first business after the disembarkment from the fleet had been accomplished was to establish an observatory at Sydney. As a site for this he chose the point on the western side of Sydney Cove, and as a compliment to the Astronomer Royal he called the place "Maskelyne Point". The first settlers and the officers of the fleet, however, had little knowledge of and no interest in that official, and much preferred to speak of "Mr. Dawes' Point"; so in due time "Maskelyne" disappeared and to-day we have "Dawes Point".

If Lieutenant Dawes was 'much engrossed with the stars' we can say of the man after whom the other point was named that James Milson was 'much engrossed with the earth.' He made a living and eventually a fortune from tilling and owning portion of the earth.

The history of Milson's Point begins on April 26, 1800, when Governor Hunter issued a grant to Robert Ryan of 120 acres of land 'on the North Shore of the Harbour opposite Sydney Cove.' A curious shifting of a place name is disclosed when one reads that the grant is to be known by the name of Hunter's Hill. In 1806 Robert Campbell, 'of the wharf', became the owner of this grant, and he altered its name to 'Carabella.' James Milson arrived in Sydney about 1804, and a few years later he settled at Parramatta. In 1823 he appears on the estimates for the colony as 'Keeper of Government House, Sydney,' at a salary of 2/per day. Another curious alteration of names occurs in connection with the name Milson. This name is almost invariably spelt "Milsom" in old documents, in the early directories of Sydney and on the maps of Sydney Harbour. Apparently Mr Milson's position permitted him to follow other occupations, for we find that in the year 1822 Robert Campbell leased the grant on the North Shore to him for eight years at an annual rental of £8… Mr Milson started a dairy farm there and made a success of it. His principal customers were the ships in the harbour and each morning a boat set out to deliver the milk to the ships. Another source of revenue was the "Milk House" which we should designate "Refreshment Room." A row across the harbour, a walk through the bush, and refreshments at the "Milk House" were one of Sydney's mild Sunday amusements a hundred years ago.

It was a natural thing that the point where the visitors landed, and from which Mr Milson's produce was shipped, should receive his name, and one feels that the railway station on the brow of the point fittingly perpetuates the name of the pioneer.

Extract from "Dawes and Milson – Men Who Gave Their Names to Bridge Ends" *by C.H. Bertie*

Supplement to the Sydney Morning Herald, Saturday March 19, 1932, page 3

OPPOSITE: Highest point on Bridge climb

Opposite: Mural, Cumberland Street

Dancing, Kirribilli side

59

The entrance to South East Pylon

Then came the war; and after the war a period when borrowing was fatally easy. In the boom conditions which then prevailed it was much simpler to persuade Parliament to authorise the vast expenditure than it had been before; J.H. Cann, as Minister for Works, had twice put authorising bills though the Assembly, to see them thrown out by the Council. In the work of preparing these bills Dr Bradfield had taken a foremost part. His original scheme was for a cantilever bridge. After a world tour in 1922 he was satisfied that a bridge of the arch type was feasible: and the necessary Act having been passed – it was carried through by R.T. Ball – the tenders invited allowed for alternative designs, either arch or cantilever. While the matter was before Parliament, Bradfield almost lived on the premises. The Minister made a speech or two on the floor of the house; Bradfield made a hundred in the lobbies and the party rooms.

Six firms submitted 20 tenders; and on May 24, 1924, the tender of Dorman, Long and Co. Ltd., for an arch-type bridge, to cost £4,217,721 11. 10d., was accepted – this exclusive of approaches.

Extract from "The Men Who Talked the Bridge"

The Bulletin, March 23, 1932, page 3

Workshop, Middlemiss Street, Milsons Point

Milsons Point Station

Alfred Street, Milsons Point

Moonscape

Too frequently is the average Australian prone to accept genius on the part of a fellow-native with little more than scant recognition. In other countries, the greatly favored in natural gifts are boosted to the limit, and rightly become figures of immortal national adulation.

For instance, few of us realise, or do not think of the remarkable mental capacity of John Job Crew Bradfield, the brilliant brain whose splendid creative work has tangible expression in the great Sydney Harbour Bridge. Once one gives more than a cursory interest to the giant structure, its majestic beauty and overpowering solidity, one is quick to halt in an overwhelming feeling of admiration. As you rest in the shadows of massive girders you think of the great achievement of man in many fields, the miracle of the Pyramids of Egypt; the Pylons, each 285 feet high, on a base of 222 feet by 162 feet, a modern challenge to Cheops !

Truly the Bridge is an undeniable creation of genius; J.J.C. Bradfield, a brilliant scholar and an engineer without peer in his profession, is rich in those gifts which are the lot of only the chosen few.

Extract from "An Australian Genius"

The Sydney Harbour Bridge Times, February 17, 1934, page 14

68

Goodyear Blimp

'Sydney can boast, even in these chequered times, that she has built for posterity,' says the Sunday Observer, in a tribute to the opening of the Sydney Harbor Bridge.

'The bridge, both in itself and its symbolism,' says the newspaper, 'is fulfilling the aspiration to make a man's achievement give unity to the work of nature.'

The Sunday Times, in a leading article, says 'Standing where the first settlers erected their huts in 1788, it is both a superb achievement and symbol of another superb achievement – the making of a nation.'

Extract from "A Nation is Now Built – Britain's View of the Bridge" LONDON, Sunday

The Daily Telegraph, Monday March 21, 1932, page 1

OPPOSITE: *View from Ultimo, 9 a.m.*

The Executive Council yesterday approved of the tolls and charges to be payable in respect of traffic over the Sydney Harbour Bridge. They will come into operation at midnight on Saturday.

Motor cars and motor cycles with sidecars, including the drivers, will be charged /6 each, and a charge of /3 will be made for each adult (other than the driver) travelling on these vehicles. Each child in a vehicle will be charged /1.

The following is the schedule of tolls and charges under the regulations;-

Motor cars and motor cycles with side-cars attached. /6 each.

Bicycles, tricycles, and motor cycles without side-car. /3 each.

Sulkies and four-wheeled buggies and light carts, hand propelled or drawn by one or more horses. /3 each.

Empty or loaded vans, lorries, drays, waggons, or other vehicles, the tare weight of which does not exceed 2 tons, 1/ each. Empty or loaded vans, lorries, drays, waggons, or other vehicles, the tare weight of which exceeds 2 tons, but does not exceed 3 tons, 2/ each.

Vehicles not otherwise specified. 3/ each.

Horse and rider. /3.

Horses or cattle (loose stock), per head. /2.

Sheep or pigs, per head. /1.

Where a second vehicle is attached to any of the above vehicles, double the specified rates will be charged.

Persons riding in or on any vehicle (other than the person driving such vehicle), will be charged /3 for each adult, and /1 for each child.

View from Pyrmont Bridge, 9 p.m.

Sydney Harbor appeared like a fairyland last night, with the Bridge like a string of stars from the city to the North Shore.

For the first time the lighting of the Harbour Bridge was tested, and the effect was extraordinary. Ferry travellers, who, in the future, will accept it as a matter of course, acclaimed it last night as a magnificent spectacle.

The lights of the bridge roadway and the near approaches were used, and they provided a brilliant flare.

During the trial the steamer Aldington Court, loaded with wheat for Dakar, left its berth. It was the first ship to pass under the illuminated bridge.

Dr Bradfield, Mr Myers, and other engineers watched the experiment, which was a complete success.

The illumination was heralded by blasts on the siren at Dawes Point, and some ferry passengers were alarmed until the blaze of light furnished the explanation.

Bridge Lights – String of Stars Across Harbor

The Daily Telegraph, Saturday January 9, 1932, page 5

OPPOSITE: Pier One, Dawes Point

Lavender Street turnoff, Milsons Point

Moving past the toll gates, heading south

Opposite: Milsons Point, looking to Dawes Point

The interior of the Pylon is equivalent in size to a 10-storied office block.

- SEE THE ROOFTOP AND LOOKOUT. Breathtaking panorama of Sydney and its environs. A glorious five-million acre view from 300 feet above the Harbour, with good visibility up to 100 miles. The best vantage point from which to see Sydney – A PHOTOGRAPHER'S PARADISE.
- WORLD FAMOUS WHITE CATS. A joy for the kiddies and a delight for adults. They are unique; they even have their own merry-go-round !
- GIANT ELECTRIC BINOCULARS AND TELESCOPES enable you to see perfectly the finest view in the world. The whole of Sydney laid before your eyes.
- THE LARGEST MAP OF NSW ever built. A scale of four miles to the inch.
- PHOTOGRAPHER. Have a souvenir photograph taken against a backdrop of the Bridge in the Pylon studio. INSTANT PROCESSING
- UNUSUAL SOUVENIRS. Australian made and first-rate quality. Your choice of more than 1,500 low-priced lines in Sydney's highest shop. ALL TYPES OF FILMS IN STOCK.
- LUNCHEON, TEAS. The PYLON TEA-ROOMS serve delicious Pylon-made refreshments. Enjoy a home-cooked luncheon overlooking a beautiful vista of the Harbour.

You can also buy ice cream, chocolates, cigarettes and icy cold fruit drinks at the BUFFET in the PYLON.

Extract from "Pylon Lookout" circa 1960's

Held in Stanton Library Local History Collection

Lori and Bev Armitage with Gus, Milsons Point

Corporate Triathlon, Pier One

Corporate Triathlon, Farm Cove

84

The Wentworth, Sydney's most up to date hotel is ideally situated overlooking the southern approach to the Sydney Harbour Bridge. Away from city noises and dust it has the advantage of being handy to all shops, theatres and the business centre. Wentworth conveniences include hot and cold water; telephone in each room; the hotel is heated during winter; and has cool air during summer. The Wentworth cuisine is excellent, and the tariff is moderate.

Visit Sydney for This Occasion and Stay at the Wentworth

Advertisement from The Sydney Mail, Wednesday January 13, 1932, page 4

QE2, *Circular Quay*

Saturday sailing, Neutral Bay

View from Mosman ferry

MORUYA GRANITE

Now Sydney's got its harbour… the problem was to span it,
Then someone said, 'Let's build a bridge, we'll use Moruya granite'.
Those pylons will be good and strong, they'll withstand any strain,
Then we can cross from side to side, on buses, cars and trains!
They've used it in St.Mary's (that cathedral up the road)
On Sydney's G.P.O. as well; I'm sure 'twill take the load.

From Scotland came the stonemasons… (a team of ninety strong),
They brought their skill across the world, to work for Dorman Long.
The Manager, John Gilmore, told them, 'Lads, you won't be sorry…
You'll think you're back in Aberdeen , when you work Moruya
   Quarry
'Cos the granite here is just as fine, as you've left back there.'
They brought Italian tradesmen too, the quarry work to share.

CHORUS
We've come from bonnie Scotland, helping Aussies build their bridge,
In Granitetown, we've made our homes, on the great blue granite ridge.
We've over 60 houses, a school-house and a store,
The Caledonian Society, has got the grandest floor…
It's West Australian jarrah-wood; we spring on toe and heel,
We're teaching all the locals, to dance the Scottish Reel.

We're teaching local lads our trade, and how to cut the granite,
Two hundred forty men employed, 44 hour week they plan it.
Each huge stone block we cut to size – within 1/8 an inch,
Each block will have a special place, those 4 pylons to clinch.
In all they'll be a total, 20,000 cubic feet.
All cut with great precision, that huge jigsaw to complete.

From "Not Forgotten: Memorials in Granite"

by Christine Greig, 1993

Words and Music by D. Philip (of Moruya)

88

Circular Quay

The man who first suggested an arch over the harbor was no engineer, but a poet who never saw Sydney except with the eye of fancy. Dr Erasmus Darwin, grandfather of the great scientist, writing in 1788, only a few months after Governor Phillip had landed his first little band of convicts at Port Jackson, used these remarkable words:

'Where Sydney Cove her lucid bosom swells,
Courts her young navies and the storm repels,
High on a rock amid the troubled air,
Hope stood sublime and wav'd her golden hair…
"Hear me," she cried, "ye rising realms! Record
Time's opening scenes and Truth's unerring word.
There, ray'd from cities o'er the cultured land,
Shall bright canals and solid roads expand;
There the proud arch, Colossus-like, bestride
Yon glittering stream and bound the chafing tide;
Embellished villas crown the landscape scene,
Farms wave with gold and orchards blush between".'

It might be going rather too far to suggest that, with his poet's eye, Dr Erasmus Darwin saw the "proud arch, Colossus-like," bestride the "glittering stream" that flows between Dawes Point and Milson's; but that at so very early a stage he should have thought of a "proud arch" at all is the more remarkable in view of the very inauspicious beginnings of the new settlement which Governor Phillip had just set up with so much sweat and travail and misgiving.

Extract from "The Men Who Talked the Bridge"

The Bulletin, Wednesday March 23, 1932, page 31

OPPOSITE: Mosman Ferry

Darling Street Wharf, Balmain East

How many will be Bridgets or Archies ? At least 30 new arrivals shared March 19, 1932, as an initial birthday.

Four girls and four boys uttered their first baby cries at St. Margaret's Hospital.

Will the parents of the girls call them Bridget ? The boys are subject to being named Jack (after Mr Lang), Lawrence, after Mr Ennis, Brad, or plain Archie, after the mighty arch.

Crown Street Women's Hospital had 12 newcomers, while at Royal North Shore two baby girls were born.

Rose, after Ald. Primrose, Mayor of North Sydney, is suggested as one baby's name.

Let it be hoped that boys are spared "Jack de Groot Bridges," or the girls, "Bridget Primrose Pylon."

Extract from "Bridge Baby Names"

The Daily Telegraph, Monday March 21, 1932, page 1

'Twas in nineteen hundred and thirty-two, on a morning in March, when the skies were blue, that the animals in Taronga Zoo heard sounds of jubilation, and the elephant cried 'Hip, hip, hooray, they are opening the Harbour Bridge to-day, in our wonderful city across the bay; let us join in the jollification'.

The Zoo Celebrates

The Sydney Morning Herald, Saturday March 19, 1932, page 9

OPPOSITE: Bradleys Head

View to Anzac Bridge from Observatory Hill

Ibis flight, from top of Bridge

If we are any judge, the Harbor Bridge is in great danger to-day. Between 10 a.m., and 3 p.m., 50,000 school children will cross in an almost continuous stream.

Having in mind our own school days, if there is anything left of the Bridge after that it doesn't matter who opens it.

On each girder will be inscribed things like 'Skinny, the Tell-tale,' 'Our Teacher is a Big Mug,' and 'Fatty Lee couldn't hurt a flea.'

And there will be cries:-

'Please, sir – Freddy Johnson is cutting his initials in the pylon.'

'Now ! Now ! Hughie ! You mustn't pull the planking up off the roadway. That's very naughty of you.'

'But I want it !'

'Miss ! Do little girls who fall off bridges always come up for the third time – because Mavis Anderson didn't.'

'Marshall ! Put that down! Stay in after school and write, three hundred times, 'I must not bend the railway lines.' '

'Please, teacher, may I leave the Bridge…?'

Of course, things may have altered since we were a boy.

"Teacher is a Big Mug, Said Kids – Watch for Initials on Pylons – Bridge Dangers" by L. W. Lower

The Daily Telegraph, Wednesday March 16, 1932, page 7

98

Pier 8, Millers Point

OPPOSITE: Alpacas returning from the Easter Show, Observatory Hill

Moreton Bay fig, Glebe Point; Baobab tree, Royal Botanic Gardens

Sumo wrestler, Sydney Cove Terminal

While the opening was spectacular in every sense of the word… one minor incident provided such controversy and amusement that it has since entered Australian folk-lore. An unknown Irishman, Francis De Groot, rode into history when he attempted to prevent Premier Lang from opening the bridge.

De Groot had moved to Australia after World War I. When Sydney solicitor Eric Campbell established an organisation known as the New Guard in 1931, De Groot became an active member. With the world starting to shake with reverberations of the Russian Revolution 15 years earlier, some (including the New Guard) saw Lang's schemes as communist-inspired and moving along the road to revolution in New South Wales.

Because of their disagreement with and dislike for Premier Lang, the New Guard was dismayed when it was announced that he was officially to open the Bridge. They believed that the only person to open a Bridge of such importance in the Empire should be a member of the Royal Family or the Governor. They immediately announced they would stop Lang from opening the Bridge.

As the big day grew closer, there were rumours that the New Guard was going to stage a coup, kidnap Lang or dump him in the harbour. What actually happened turned out to be an anti-climax and did little more than provide amusement on the one hand, and dismay on the other, among those in the nearby crowd.

By riding behind the Governor-General's cavalry guard, De Groot managed to arrive at the ceremony undetected and took up position quite close to where the ribbon would be stretched.

As the official party approached, De Groot galloped forward and slashed the ribbon with his sword, declaring the Bridge open in the name of the "decent citizens of New South Wales".

He was unceremoniously pulled from his horse by the police and taken to the Reception House, a psychiatric hospital. Some days later, after being declared sane, De Groot was fined the maximum penalty of £5, with £4 costs, for offensive behaviour on Bradfield Highway, a public place. Charges of damaging a ribbon to the extent of £2, and of using threatening words, were dismissed.

At the ceremony, the ribbon was hurriedly tied back together and everything proceeded on schedule without further interruption.

Extract from "The De Groot Incident"

From "The Story of the Sydney Harbour Bridge", page 17

Dawes Point Park

Opposite: Joey Hopper, Observatory Park, Millers Point

When the contractors hand over the Harbor Bridge to the Government they will supply a list of do's and don'ts.

Mr Lawrence Ennis, director of construction for Dorman, Long, and Co. Ltd., stated yesterday that the structure was a triumph of engineering, but as much, if not more, care would have to be taken with it after completion as during construction.

In fact, the Bridge will require as much attention as a normal mother gives to her baby.

Mr Ennis said that all parts, with the exception of the bearings, could now be made in Australia, and there would be no necessity to send to England.

So far, the Bridge has withstood all tests. Next week the engines will be shunted off, and brooms and hoses will be used to make the deck clean for the official opening.

It is estimated that the cost of cleaning the pylons is £7,500. A big gang of men, using steel brushes, is working overtime on the job.

Just Like Baby – Needs of the Big Bridge

Cleaning cart, Fitzroy Street, Kirribilli

Lower Fort Street, The Rocks

Rose Bay

I deem it a privilege to have the opportunity of congratulating the citizens of the City of Sydney and the people of New South Wales as a whole upon the successful completion and the official opening of the great Sydney bridge – one of the wonders of the modern world.

One cannot but regret that the opening of the bridge synchronises with the greatest economic depression which the world has yet experienced. At the same time, the people who have displayed the enterprise and determination to initiate and complete such a herculean undertaking in this new country must undoubtedly prove successful in overcoming the tremendous disabilities with which they are now faced.

May I express the hope that, as both sides of the harbour have been united by the bridge, so may all classes of the people of Australia unite in a common determination to achieve prosperity again for this favoured land of ours ?

W.F. Lathlain, Lord Mayor

The Hon. Sir William Lathlain. Kt., M.L.C.

The Lord Mayor of Perth

The Sydney Mail: Special Bridge Number, Wednesday March 16, 1932, page 34

Goods Railway, Lilyfield

The Bridgeview Hotel, The Rocks

The Palisade Hotel, Millers Point

Sydney Theatre Company, Dawes Point

Practically every workman on the Harbour Bridge knew Jacko. He was the Bridge watch dog, and a proud one at that, because he is the first dog to cross the structure.

Up on the arch he looked down on all other dogs.

For years he did the rounds of the Bridge at night and day with the watchmen. He knew all the workmen, and when a stranger appeared he would bark long and loudly.

One night a watchman found the dog barking up at one of the lower chords of the Bridge on the Dawes Point side. On investigation a man was found asleep inside the chord, where it was warm and sheltered from the rain and biting westerly wind.

On dark and wet nights when the watchman's lamp was not very effective, Jacko would run backwards and forwards along the tracks to guide his master.

When feeling lonely some days, Jacko would make his way up the arch to the creeper-crane driver's cabin or would lie down beside one of the painters for company.

Jacko is equally as sorry as the workmen that the job is finished. Now the leading question so far as the workmen are concerned, is not who designed the Bridge, but who is going to have Jacko.

First Dog to Cross – Jacko Helped to Build Bridge – Sorry Now

The Daily Telegraph, Saturday March 19, 1932, page 19

LONDON, MARCH 23

A model of Sydney Harbour Bridge in butter attracted much attention at Hay's Wharf offices, where the Lord Mayor (Sir Maurice Jenks), the City Sheriffs, the Australian High Commissioner (Sir Granville Ryrie), the Agents-General, and 150 others inspected a display of the Australian butters competing for the Orient Steam Navigation Company's prize.

Sir Granville Ryrie, who presided, referred to Sydney's pride in its three "ours" – our harbour, our bridge, and our Bradman.

The Under-Secretary to the Dominions Office (Mr Malcolm Macdonald) spoke of the Government's interest in the competition and said that the results of the "Buy British" campaign were exceedingly encouraging. There was now a great voluntary movement throughout the country in favour of buying home or dominion products.

Colonel Sir Bruce Porter, commandant, during the war, of the third London general hospital, through which 17,000 Australians passed, testified to the vitamin value of Australian butter, which, he said, came from cows fed in sunny pastures, whereas Northern European cows were kept in darkness through the winter.

Harbour Bridge Modelled in Butter – Australian Product Praised

From The Sydney Morning Herald, Friday March 25, 1932, page 5

Bridge replica, Warwick Farm

Johnstons Creek, Annandale

Garden, Lane Cove

ACKNOWLEDGMENTS

Pages 2, 26, 40, 43, 44, 52, 60, 71, 75, 84, 90, 93, 108, 112, and 117 – held in the State Reference Library, State Library of New South Wales

Pages 12, 30, 36, 54, 72, 94, and 118 – source: The Sydney Morning Herald

Pages 20, 29, and 38 – reproduced with the permission of The Sydney Morning Herald

Page 16 – reproduced with the permission of the Mitchell Library, State Library of New South Wales – extract from The Great Northern Bridge Opening, Souvenir, March 18, 1932

Page 22 – "Via the Bridge" by Ricketty Kate (Minnie Agnes Filson), was written in 1939 and this rendition is taken from "Sydney's Poems", Primavera Press, with acknowledgment

Page 41 and 104 – reproduced with the permission of the Roads and Traffic Authority of NSW

Page 48 – source: The Sunday Telegraph, Sunday, January 19, 1992

Page 65 – reproduced with the permission of the Mitchell Library, State Library of New South Wales – extract from The Sydney Harbour Bridge Times, February 17, 1934

Page 80 – reproduced courtesy Stanton Library Local Studies Collection

Page 88 – Mrs Dorothy Philip's poem, "Moruya Granite" published with the kind permission of Mr Hilton Philip, and with thanks also to Mrs H. Greig

Thanks also to: David Grinston, The Chapman Family, John Andrew, Alan Davies, Charlotte Snedden, Michael Jackson, Don Willey, The Porter Family, Lori and Bev Armitage, Leonie Masson, Bridge Climb, Warren Bartetzko.

Published by Peribo Pty Limited
ACN 002 273 761
58 Beaumont Road
Mount Kuring-Gai NSW 2080 Australia

© Copyright Peribo Pty Limited 1999
First edition published December 1999

All rights reserved. No part of this publication may be reproduced, stored in a retrieval system, or transmitted, in any form or by any means, electronic, mechanical, photocopying, recording or otherwise, without the prior permission in writing of the publisher, or for particular images, the individual photographers.

While all care is taken in compiling this publication, the editor and publisher assume no responsibility for the effects arising therein.

ISBN 1 86322 014 3
Printed in China

PHOTOGRAPHY: Robert Billington
RESEARCH: Sarah Billington
DESIGN: Design Smiths
PHOTOGRAPHIC PRINTING: Warren Bartetzko

All photographs were taken by Robert Billington between 1993 and 1999, using a Nikon F3 and a Rolleiflex Twin Lens Reflex, and Kodak T-max film 400.

INDEX